The MUSHROOM COOKBOOK

The MUSHROOM COOKBOOK

Victoria Lloyd-Davies

SMITHMARK

A SALAMANDER BOOK

© Salamander Books Ltd, 1992, 1994

This edition published in 1994 by
SMITHMARK Publishers Inc.,
16 East 32nd Street,
New York, NY 10016.

SMITHMARK books are available for bulk purchase for sales
promotion and premium use. For details write or call the
manager of special sales, SMITHMARK Publishers Inc.,
16 East 32nd Street, New York, NY 10016; (212) 532-6600.

ISBN: 0-8317-5864-3

CREDITS

Editor: Will Steeds
Designer: Louise Bruce
Photographer: Simon Butcher
Home economist: Wendy Dines
US consultants: Jeanette Egan, Laura Phelps,
John H. D. Rockwell
Stylist: Marian Price
Copy editor: Alison Leach
Index: Alison Leach
Typesetting: SX Composing Ltd., England
Color Separation: P&W Graphics Pte. Ltd., Singapore
Printed in Belgium

As seasoning is a matter of personal taste, salt and pepper have
not been listed in the ingredients.

Contents

Foreword

by Antonio Carluccio

There are two good reasons for me to write the foreword to this book. First, because it deals with mushrooms and, although I am fanatical about wild mushrooms, I also appreciate and love the cultivated varieties. Second, but no less important, because I know that Victoria Lloyd-Davies has dedicated a great part of her life to the good cause of the mushroom.

Victoria is very interested in the mycological field, and with this book she demonstrates that besides commercial professionalism there is also an emotional part of herself ready to share a passion for loving and cooking this natural little wonder. I call mushrooms this because they still, whether cultivated or not, represent a sort of magic in the complexity of the botanical world.

Many mysteries are still to be discovered in the infinite mushroom world. For example, it is indeed intriguing to think about how a mushroom is constructed, how it reproduces and how it does so, so quickly. For mushrooms aren't able to use the sun's rays to nourish themselves like so many other plants – photosynthesis doesn't take place, as mushrooms contain no chlorophyll. All the energy and food for growing is taken from other matter.

The mystery lies in how mushrooms are transformed into something so very enjoyable and precious – like wine and bread, for example – from such matter. For it must be said that on top of taste and versatility in cooking they also represent one of the best forms of nourishment, low in fat and calories, high in proteins and minerals.

I jokingly used to say that cultivated mushrooms were bland compared to the wild variety. But in a world from which dozens of wild mushrooms disappear annually from the natural scene, it is most important not to joke any more about cultivated mushrooms but to appreciate the incredible work and research done by thousands of people all over the world to improve their quality still further. Their dedication means that we get more varieties, and of better quality, which we will be able to enjoy for a long time to come.

There are many books about cooking with wild mushrooms, but few about creating meals using cultivated ones. The Mushroom Cookbook, full of valuable advice and suggestions for the better understanding of the culinary values of cultivated mushrooms, fills this gap admirably. The recipes are all fabulous and easy to prepare. It is intriguing how Victoria can turn an innocent button into a sort of devil, or arrange perfect marriages with fish, meat and cheese.

An important aspect of this book is how it talks about the preparation of mushrooms in a healthy way as either a starter or a main course for everybody, vegetarian or not.

Author's Introduction

There is no doubt that wild mushrooms picked in the fields in the early morning and cooked for breakfast are a great treat. Yet finding the right mushrooms is a specialist's task with dire consequences for those who make the wrong choice.

It is all too easy for the inexperienced to make mistakes and pick the wrong mushrooms. The white cap mushrooms (Agaricus bisporus), generally seen in stores today, are a very close relation to the field mushroom (Agaricus campestris), the wood mushroom (Agaricus silviola), and the horse mushroom (Agaricus arvensis). Cultivated mushrooms are 100 percent safe to eat, and unlike their wild relations, which grow mainly in the spring and fall and are killed off by frost, are available fresh every day of the year.

Mushroom growers, whether they have just small farms or are responsible for production on a massive scale, aim to replicate the same natural conditions that make mushrooms grow in the wild. They know that the consumer demands quality and different varieties of fresh mushrooms.

This book is a collection of almost a hundred recipes which I have created with the aim of helping you to make the most of mushrooms in your cookery. The recipes range from the simplest of snacks – mushrooms on toast – to dishes which will delight your dinner guests; from quick and nutritious starters and salads to equally fast stir-fries; from comforting soups for a cold winter evening to kebabs cooked on a barbecue on a hot summer day. You will find traditional steak and mushroom pie or a modern mushroom and tomato pie made with filo pastry. There are also recipes for vegetarians and vegans which will be just as popular with non-vegetarians.

There is still a mystique about mushrooms, so I have included information about the buying, storing and preparation of mushrooms, explaining the differences in size and maturity of the white mushroom and introducing you to some of the cultivated specialty mushrooms now easily available. I have recommended a particular type of mushroom for each recipe but this is primarily a matter of personal choice. If, for instance, you prefer the tightly closed small buttons rather than large white mushrooms, then use them instead in the recipes.

All the recipes use ingredients which are readily available and most are quick and easy to prepare.

Cultivated mushrooms can be used to make hundreds of different dishes. Put them on your weekly shopping list and enjoy making the recipes in this book.

Victore Lloyd-Davies

Introduction

THE CULTIVATED MUSHROOM

Cultivated mushrooms are one of the most valuable horticultural crops. A high proportion of the fresh mushrooms sold in food stores is the white mushroom known as *Agaricus bisporus*. These are classified in three grades or sizes: small buttons, medium buttons, and large white mushrooms. The others are specialty mushrooms. Brown or crimini mushrooms are similar to the white mushroom apart from their color; and they have a firmer texture and nutty flavor. They are available either as medium buttons or large mushrooms. Oyster mushrooms, which are fan-shaped, are generally brown, but some are slate-gray, yellow or pink. Shiitake mushrooms are umbrella-like with dark brown caps and delicate white gills showing underneath. Enoki mushrooms have long, thin white stems, topped with tiny "buttons."

GROWING CULTIVATED MUSHROOMS

Mushrooms are not a new vegetable. People have been eating them for centuries. The Pharaohs thought they were food from heaven; the Romans enjoyed them and they were considered a feast in the fall from the Middle Ages to the Renaissance.

The first written accounts of how to grow cultivated mushrooms date from around 1650. Mushroom cultivation originated in France where they were grown in caves. Today, cultivated mushrooms are grown all year round in environmentally controlled growing houses on farms throughout the world.

The mushroom is the fruit body of a fungus. It grows from long, fine, white-gray threads (mycelium) in specially prepared compost. The compost comes from local sources such as farms and is pasteurized to become a sweet-smelling, inert and natural medium for the growing fruit bodies. As both the temperature and humidity can now be controlled by the growers, we are able to eat mushrooms throughout the year. Mushrooms are grown naturally. Each crop takes about six weeks to mature, ready for picking – usually by hand.

Most mushroom farms grow the white cap *Agaricus bisporus*. Many people are under the misapprehension that the three sizes of *Agaricus bisporus* are three different varieties. This is not so.

9

The mushroom doubles in size every 24 hours, so over a period of a week, a small button will develop into a medium button, with its gills visible, and finally will become a large white mushroom. As the size increases, the full mature flavor develops.

The brown or crimini mushroom is grown like the *Agaricus bisporus,* but the strain is slightly different, producing a mushroom with a brown outer skin.

Oyster mushrooms are cultivated on straw which is enclosed in black plastic bags. The grower makes holes in the bags, and the mushrooms are thus encouraged to grow in clusters outside the bags, emulating their natural habitat on the trunks of trees.

Shiitake mushrooms were first grown in China and Japan. They used to be cultivated on dead or dying deciduous tree logs in Japan but today they are mostly grown on blocks of sawdust contained in a plastic mesh.

The grower decides when to pick the mushrooms according to the demands of the food stores or wholesale markets in meeting the needs of the consumer or caterer. Mushrooms are in the food stores the day after they have been picked.

CHOOSING THE RIGHT MUSHROOM

First choose the right grade or size of mushroom for your recipe.

The small button mushrooms have a delicate flavor and firm texture. They can be eaten raw in salads, served as a crudité for dips, used as a decorative garnish and are ideal for including in pale-colored sauces.

Medium button mushrooms are still firm and white but double the size of small buttons. They can be eaten raw or cooked. They are probably the most popular mushroom. They can be marinated lightly for salads, threaded onto metal kebab skewers for barbecues, cooked whole with fish and chicken or sliced for pizzas or quiches.

The larger ones are more mature in flavor, and the gills can be seen under the caps. These are ideal for making garlic mushrooms or broiling as a vegetable, making soups and casseroles, or teaming with red meats and game.

The large white mushrooms are fully mature with a rich flavor.

The veil is partly broken on the larger button mushrooms, with pinkish gills visible under the cap. The mushrooms still retain their cup shape.

Large white mushrooms have a completely broken veil; the gills are a darker brown, and the cap of the mushroom is flatter. The mushroom is "T"-shaped. They range in size from around 2 inches upward.

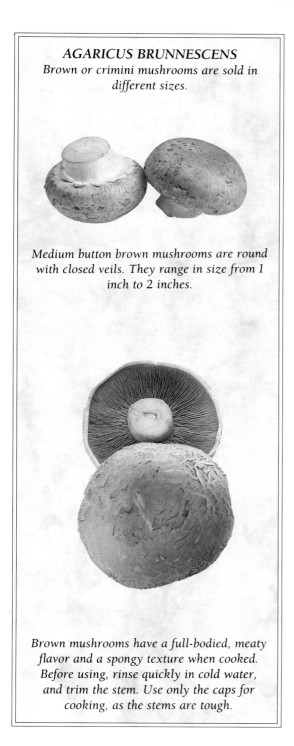

AGARICUS BRUNNESCENS
Brown or crimini mushrooms are sold in different sizes.

Medium button brown mushrooms are round with closed veils. They range in size from 1 inch to 2 inches.

Brown mushrooms have a full-bodied, meaty flavor and a spongy texture when cooked. Before using, rinse quickly in cold water, and trim the stem. Use only the caps for cooking, as the stems are tough.

They can range from around 2 inches in diameter up to the size of a dinner plate. They are perfect for stuffing with different mixtures, or for slicing and cooking with steak or pan-broiled bacon and eggs. Their flavor also makes them ideal to use in stuffings for a roast.

Brown mushrooms, also known as crimini or Italian or Roman brown mushrooms, are tan to dark brown with a deep, earthy flavor. They have a richer flavor and meatier texture than white mushrooms. They hold their shape well when cooked, and do not release as much moisture.

Oyster mushrooms are beige, cream or gray with fluted caps that resemble a fan or oyster shell. They are also referred to as *pleurottes, pleurotes* or *pleurotus*. They have a delicate flavor and texture. They can be eaten raw, but are usually cooked. They can be used whole or sliced, and can replace white mushrooms in most recipes, particularly stir-fries, fish dishes and in creamy sauces. They are good fried, broiled or baked.

Shiitake mushrooms, also referred to as oak, Chinese or Black Forest mushrooms, are tan to dark brown with a large open veil between the stem and the cap. They contain twice as much protein as white mushrooms, and have a unique steak-like texture and meaty flavor. They can be eaten raw, in which case you will detect a faint peppery bite, but they are generally cooked. Their slightly slippery texture particularly enhances Chinese and oriental dishes. Their strong flavor makes them the ideal choice for special dark mushroom sauces; shiitake and Madeira are perfect partners.

Enoki mushrooms have long, thin white stems joined at the base, and a tiny "button" on top. They have a light mild flavor and crisp texture. Toss raw enoki in salads, tuck into sandwiches, and use as a garnish for soups.

BUYING AND STORING MUSHROOMS

Fresh mushrooms need careful handling. If treated roughly, they can bruise and valuable nutrients will be lost.

Take care when selecting mushrooms in a store. Handle them as little as possible and avoid putting any heavy items on top of them in your shopping basket or supermarket cart.

Mushrooms should be stored in the salad drawer of a refrigerator. They should never be washed before storing – just remove any plastic wrap from the package, and cover the mushrooms with a paper towel. If you have brought them home loose in a plastic bag, transfer them carefully into a paper bag. See page 15 for information on freezing mushrooms.

All mushrooms are best when eaten fresh but they will keep for a few days in a refrigerator. The different sizes of white mushrooms should be eaten within five days of purchase. Brown or crimini mushrooms last slightly longer, about a week. Oyster mushrooms will keep for three or four days, and shiitake mushrooms should be eaten within six days.

PREPARATION

Mushrooms are normally perfectly clean; any dark specks on them are peat. It is best to rinse them quickly in a strainer, under cold running water, just before you eat or cook them, and then pat dry with a paper towel.

Never peel cultivated mushrooms or remove their stalks. The whole mushroom is edible and the skin contains nutrients and flavor. The mushroom is a single structure so it is damaged if the stalk is pulled out. If you like stuffed mushrooms, trim the stalk back slightly, then mold the stuffing around the stalk, using it as a firm support.

Cultivated mushrooms can be eaten raw or cooked. They can be eaten whole, sliced thickly, halved or quartered. Always slice mushrooms downward through the cap to the stalk, using a sharp pointed knife. At this stage a sprinkling of lemon juice will help to retain the delicate pale color of small or medium buttons.

NUTRITION

Mushrooms are an important part of a healthy diet. The full nutritional value is obtained when the mushrooms are eaten raw or lightly cooked.

- **Low in calories**
  Less than 30 calories per ¼ pound. Useful in low-calorie diets as mushrooms also provide some fiber which promotes the "satiety" factor.

PLEUROTUS

Oyster mushrooms are fan-shaped and vary in size from 3⅜ inches to 5 inches. They grow in clusters of overlapping tiers, like roof tiles. They vary in color from dark brown to slate-gray, and some are bright yellow. The gills are white, and they have short, solid stems.

Pleurotus ostreatus – gray oyster mushrooms

Pleurotus pulmonarius – dark brown oyster mushrooms

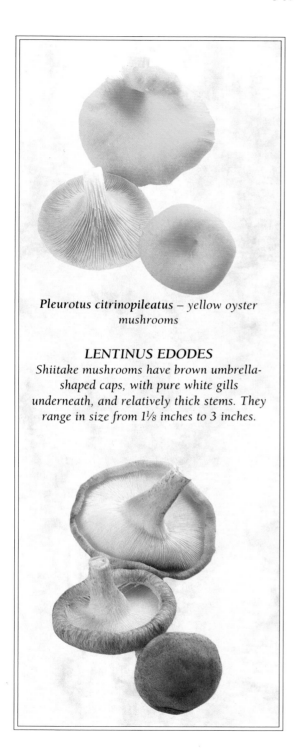

Pleurotus citrinopileatus – yellow oyster mushrooms

LENTINUS EDODES

Shiitake mushrooms have brown umbrella-shaped caps, with pure white gills underneath, and relatively thick stems. They range in size from 1⅛ inches to 3 inches.

■ **Low in fat and no cholesterol**
Excellent eating for a healthy heart.

■ **Low in salt**
Solves the taste problem of a low-salt diet. Mushrooms add flavor to food cooked without salt.

■ **Good source of minerals**
Particularly potassium, which is a great asset to the elderly as their diet tends to be restricted.

■ **Good source of vitamins**
Vegans should note that mushrooms and yeast are their sole sources of vital B12.

■ **Vegetable protein**
Mushrooms are an excellent source of vegetable proteins because they contain several of the essential amino acids. *Agaricus bisporus*, the white mushroom, ranks above all other vegetables, except beans, peas and lentils, in its essential amino acid content. Between 70 and 90 percent of the vegetable protein present can be easily digested.

AGARICUS BISPORUS		
	Average value per ¼ pound	
	Energy	30 calories
	Protein	3g
	Fat	0.2g
	Cholesterol	nil
	Sugar	trace
VITAMINS	B1 (Thiamine)	0.1mg
	B2 (Riboflavin)	0.4mg
	Niacin	0.5mg
	Pantothenic Acid	6.2mg
	Folic Acid	0.016mg
	B12	0.05mg
	Vitamin C	2mg
MINERALS	Phosphorus	75mg
	Potassium	620mg
	Iron	1mg
	Copper	1mg
	Zinc	0.86mg
	Selinium	Trace
	Salt	6mg
	Dietary Fiber	1g

COOKING WITH MUSHROOMS

- The average portion of raw mushrooms is ¼ pound. As a cooked vegetable, allow 6 ounces.

- Sliced button mushrooms are excellent for sandwich fillings.

- Dip button mushrooms into cheese fondue for a meal or into natural yogurt for a snack.

- The larger the mushrooms, the more mature the flavor. They complement meat and game.

- Trimmed mushroom stalks should be used to make stocks and consommés.

- Brown mushrooms have a higher percentage of dry matter. They are excellent when making mushroom pâtés, breads and pastries.

- A few large white mushrooms may be put into the roasting pan around a roast or a chicken for the last 10 minutes of cooking.

- Mushrooms can be cooked on the stove top, under a broiler, or in an oven or microwave.

- Mushrooms should always be cooked quickly, particularly when frying them – otherwise, they will absorb all the fat and lose their flavor.

- Mushrooms do not need long cooking. Add them to casseroles for the last 20 minutes.

- Quartered or roughly chopped mushrooms make a good alternative to ground beef for vegetarians.

- Choose small or medium button mushrooms to "turn" for special occasions. Make a series of curved cuts from the top of each mushroom cap to the base. Remove a narrow strip of peel along each cut. See page 61.

- Sliced mushrooms make an attractive garnish for other dishes; soups, broiled fish or steaks.

- Specialty mushrooms have lovely shapes and colors – excellent for entertaining.

- Mushrooms make "alternative" starters. Coat them with seafood dressing and serve instead of shrimp cocktail. Poach them in white wine, then toss them in garlic butter and serve instead of snails with crusty bread.

- Medium button mushrooms should always be marinated well before barbecuing.

- The large brown or crimini mushrooms, stuffed and wrapped in foil, cook well on barbecues.

- Raw mushrooms taste delicious in salads but if you prefer the texture of cooked mushrooms, poach them for 5 minutes in wine or fruit juice, then chill them in the liquid.

- Marinated mushrooms keep well for five days in an airtight container in the refrigerator, making them an ideal vegetable to prepare ahead for dinner parties, or celebration buffets.

- Bargain hunters can often buy bulk supplies from local farm shops. It is best to freeze mushrooms sliced rather than whole. Sauté sliced mushrooms lightly and quickly in a little butter or oil. Drain them on paper towels. Open freeze the mushrooms on trays, then transfer them into freezer bags. Store for up to three months. Use straight from the freezer for pies and casseroles.

- For every 1 pound of mushrooms, allow ¼ cup of butter and ½ cup of chopped shallots to make duxelle. Cook the chopped mushrooms and shallots in the butter over a moderate heat, stirring occasionally, until all the liquid has evaporated and the mixture is dry. Season lightly. Pack into ice-cube trays and freeze until firm. Then transfer the cubes of duxelle into freezer bags. Store for up to three months. Use like stock cubes to flavor gravy, soups, sauces and stuffings.

- Mushrooms can also be pickled and preserved in oil. See recipe on page 78.

Soups and Starters

Mushroom soup can be light and creamy in color or robust and comforting.
You can make it in bulk, using less liquid, freezing it in concentrated form
and adding the remaining liquid when it is reheated. Mushrooms make
excellent hot and cold starters. They are particularly good marinated and
chilled – ideal when entertaining as you can prepare them ahead.

Mushroom filo baskets

Grease four upturned ¾-cup ramekins (or metal molds) lightly. Drape one half sheet of filo pastry over a ramekin, brush with melted butter, and press overhanging edges back up onto the pastry on the ramekin. Cover with another half sheet of pastry, and brush with melted butter. Repeat with the remaining pastry and dishes. Place on a baking sheet, and bake in a preheated 350°F oven for 15 minutes.

To make the filling, heat the oil and cook the scallions, carrots, pepper, mushrooms, and ginger root for 5 minutes, stirring. Stir in the asparagus, bean sprouts, and soy sauce. Cook for a further 3 minutes, then pile into the pastry cases. **Serves 4**

Mushroom hors d'oeuvre

Put the mushrooms into a mixing bowl with 2 tablespoons of the lemon juice, the scallions, sunflower seeds and seasoning. Mix well, and chill. Just before serving, remove the pit and peel from the avocado, then slice the flesh, and sprinkle with the remaining lemon juice. Arrange the avocado slices on individual serving plates with the mushroom salad. **Serves 4-6**

Right: Mushroom filo baskets.

INGREDIENTS

¼ cup melted unsalted butter
4 sheets filo pastry, cut in half crosswise
FILLING
2 tablespoons oil
⅓ cup finely chopped scallions
3-4 young carrots, sliced
½ orange bell pepper, seeded and cut into small strips
½ pound small button mushrooms
1-1½ teaspoons grated ginger root
½ cup chopped thin asparagus stalks
1 cup fresh bean sprouts
2 tablespoons light soy sauce

½ pound small button mushrooms, sliced
3 tablespoons lemon juice
4 scallions, chopped
1 tablespoon sunflower seeds, toasted
1 ripe avocado

Rich mushroom soup

Melt the butter in a large saucepan, add the mushrooms and cook for 3 minutes. Add the flour, and stir well to coat the mushrooms. Stir in the vegetable stock and milk, and bring to a boil slowly. Cover the pan, and simmer for 5 minutes. Cool, then purée in a blender. Season to taste.

Chill if serving cold or reheat if serving hot. Pour into soup bowls, and stir in the cream. Garnish with parsley. **Serves 6**

Crispy chicken with mustard sauce

Combine the chicken, mushrooms, parsley and seasoning together. Shape into 16 3-inch sausages. Chill. Mix the breadcrumbs and sesame seeds together. Dip each sausage into the beaten egg, then coat with the breadcrumb mixture. Chill.

Just before serving, mix the sauce ingredients together. Deep fry the sausages for about 5 minutes, or until golden-brown and cooked through to the center. Serve with the sauce. **Serves 4**

Mushroom and seafood special

Brush a roasting pan lightly with the oil. Arrange the mushrooms, cap side down, in the roasting pan. Mix the haddock with the shrimp, breadcrumbs, oyster sauce and egg yolk. Divide the fish mixture between the mushrooms. Sprinkle the cheese on top. Bake in a preheated 400°F oven for 10 minutes. **Serves 4**

Top left: Crispy chicken with mustard sauce; Rich mushroom soup (top right); Mushroom and seafood special (bottom).

INGREDIENTS

¼ cup butter
1 pound medium button mushrooms, thickly sliced
4 tablespoons all-purpose flour
1¼ cups vegetable stock
2½ cups milk
⅔ cup light cream
GARNISH
chopped parsley

❧

½ pound chicken breast fillets, minced
½ pound large white mushrooms, very finely chopped
2 tablespoons chopped parsley
¾ cup fresh white breadcrumbs
4 tablespoons sesame seeds
1 small egg, beaten
oil for frying
SAUCE
scant 1¼ cups low-fat fromage frais
4 teaspoons horseradish mustard
1 tablespoon lemon juice

❧

1 teaspoon oil
8 large white mushrooms
½ pound haddock fillet, cut into small pieces
¼ pound peeled cooked shrimp
¾ cup fresh white breadcrumbs
1 teaspoon oyster sauce
1 egg yolk, beaten
½ cup grated Cheddar cheese

❧

Ginger, split pea and mushroom soup

Put the onion, ginger root, cilantro, split peas and stock into a saucepan. Bring to a boil, cover, and simmer gently for 30 minutes. Add the mushrooms, and simmer for a further 15 minutes. Season to taste, then serve garnished with lemon slices and sprigs of cilantro. **Serves 4-6**

Country soup

Heat the oil, and cook the onion for 1 minute. Add the mushrooms, and cook for a further minute. Stir in the stock, lemon peel and parsley. Bring to a boil, and simmer for 5 minutes. Stir in the breadcrumbs and seasoning, and cook for 1 minute. Remove from the heat, and stir in the sour cream. Reheat gently, but do not allow to boil. **Serves 6**

Mushroom chowder

Melt the butter in a large saucepan. Add the onions, celery, garlic, potatoes, and carrots, and cook for 5 minutes, stirring occasionally. Add the stock, milk, mushrooms, and haddock, and bring to a boil slowly. Add the peas and corn, and bring back to a boil slowly. Cover the pan, and simmer for 5 minutes. Season to taste. **Serves 8**

Right: Mushroom chowder.

INGREDIENTS

1 onion, finely chopped
1 tablespoon grated ginger root
2 tablespoons chopped fresh cilantro
½ pound green split peas
5 cups vegetable stock
10 ounces small button mushrooms, sliced

❧

2 tablespoons oil
1 onion, chopped
½ pound large white mushrooms, finely chopped
5 cups vegetable stock
grated peel of 1 lemon
3 tablespoons chopped parsley
1½ cups fresh whole-wheat breadcrumbs
2 tablespoons sour cream

❧

2 tablespoons butter
2 onions, finely chopped
4 stalks celery, finely chopped
1 clove garlic, finely chopped
1 pound potatoes, diced
1 cup diced carrots
2½ cups hot vegetable stock
1¼ cups milk
1 pound medium button mushrooms, quartered
½ pound haddock fillet, cut into small pieces
⅔ cup fresh or frozen green peas
8-ounce can whole-kernel corn, drained

Coriander mushrooms

Squeeze half the lemon juice over the mushrooms. Crush the coriander seeds with a rolling pin. Heat 3 tablespoons of the olive oil in a skillet, and add the crushed coriander seeds. Heat gently for a few seconds, then add the mushrooms, bay leaves and seasoning. Stir-fry for 1 minute. Cover the skillet, and cook over a low heat for 5 minutes. Transfer to a serving dish, and pour the remaining olive oil and lemon juice over the mushrooms. Serve hot or cold with crusty bread. **Serves 4**

Baked mushroom molds with tomato sauce

Heat the oil and fry the mushrooms and onion for 5 minutes, stirring occasionally. Put into a food processor, and blend until smooth. Add the remaining ingredients, and blend for 15 seconds. Turn into four large greased molds or ramekins. Cover with foil, then bake in a preheated 350°F oven for about 25 minutes until quite firm.

To make the sauce, put the ingredients into a saucepan. Bring to a boil, cover the pan, and simmer for 15 minutes. Remove the lid, then boil rapidly for about 8 minutes until the mixture is fairly thick. Press through a strainer or blend in a food processor until smooth. Return to the pan, and keep warm. Spoon the sauce onto 4 serving plates, then invert the mushroom molds on top. Garnish with sprigs of watercress. **Serves 4**

Top right: Coriander mushrooms; Baked mushroom molds with tomato sauce (bottom).

INGREDIENTS

juice of ½ lemon
1 pound brown mushrooms, quartered
1 tablespoon coriander seeds
4 tablespoons olive oil
4 bay leaves

❧

2 tablespoons oil
¾ pound large white mushrooms, chopped
1 onion, chopped
1 medium egg, beaten
3 tablespoons milk
2 teaspoons Dijon mustard
SAUCE
½ pound carrots, chopped
14-ounce can peeled chopped tomatoes
1 onion, chopped

❧

Mushroom fruit salad

Peel 1 orange, and remove the pith. Cut the orange crosswise, then into quarters. Mix with the mushrooms, slivered almonds and strawberries. Squeeze the juice from the remaining orange and the ½ lemon, and pour over the mushrooms. Arrange the cucumber around the edge of the salad bowl, and put the mushroom mixture in the center. Sprinkle with chopped mint, and garnish with a sprig of mint. Chill for 1 hour. **Serves 4**

Mushroom pâté

Melt 2 tablespoons of the butter in a skillet, and fry the onion and garlic gently until almost cooked, then add the mushrooms, and continue frying until the onion and mushrooms are cooked. Increase the heat, and cook very quickly to evaporate any liquid, stirring frequently. Season well with salt and pepper, and turn into individual dishes. Chill. Melt the remaining butter, and pour over the pâté. Chill before serving with toast. **Serves 4**

Marinated mushrooms

Put the vinegar, garlic, bay leaf and onion into a saucepan. Bring to a boil, and simmer until the onion is tender. Add the tomato paste and oil. Mix together thoroughly, and season to taste. Pour the marinade over the mushrooms, cover, and chill overnight. Remove the garlic and bay leaf. Serve in individual dishes, garnished with cilantro. **Serves 4**

Right: Marinated mushrooms.

INGREDIENTS

2 oranges
½ pound small button mushrooms
¼ cup slivered almonds
6 ounces strawberries, sliced
½ lemon
½ cucumber, sliced
1 tablespoon finely chopped fresh mint
GARNISH
sprig of mint

❧

⅔ cup butter
1 onion, finely chopped
2 cloves garlic
1 pound brown mushrooms, finely chopped
TO SERVE
triangles of toast

❧

½ cup wine vinegar
½ clove garlic
1 bay leaf
1 small onion, finely chopped
2 tablespoons tomato paste
3 tablespoons oil
1 pound small button mushrooms
GARNISH
fresh cilantro

❧

Salads

You do not have to cook mushrooms. The small crunchy button mushrooms taste delicious in salads. Rinse them in a strainer under cold running water just before you eat them. If you prefer mushrooms to be slightly softer, marinate them in French dressing for a couple of hours, or poach them lightly in a little wine and chill them, then toss them into salads.

Mushroom and alfalfa salad with garlic croûtons

Sprinkle the buttered bread lightly with the garlic powder, and toast under a preheated broiler. Cut into small cubes. Toss all the prepared vegetables together, then scatter the garlic croûtons over the top. If liked, substitute enoki mushrooms for the alfalfa sprouts. **Serves 6**

Eggs with radicchio and mushrooms

Tear the radicchio leaves into a salad bowl. Add the fennel, mushrooms, eggs and parsley. Whisk the remaining ingredients together, and pour over the salad, then toss well. **Serves 4**

Top right: Eggs with radicchio and mushrooms; Mushroom and alfalfa salad with garlic croûtons (bottom).

INGREDIENTS

4 slices white bread, buttered on both sides and crusts removed
a little garlic powder
1 pound small button mushrooms, halved
¼ pound enoki mushrooms
or
2 cups alfalfa sprouts
5 ounces radishes, quartered
½ pound daikon, chopped
celery leaves
1 Italian fennel bulb, chopped

2 small radicchio
1 Italian fennel bulb, finely sliced
¼ pound large white mushrooms, thickly sliced
6 hard-cooked eggs, quartered
1 tablespoon chopped parsley
2 tablespoons lemon juice
1 tablespoon Worcestershire sauce

Cracked wheat salad

Put the cracked wheat, wine and water into a saucepan. Cover, and bring to a boil, then simmer, uncovered, for 20 minutes or until the liquid has been absorbed.

Meanwhile, slice the mushrooms thickly and toss in the vinaigrette dressing. Core and slice the apples, and toss lightly in lemon juice. Cut the cheese into small cubes. Arrange the salad on individual plates and serve. **Serves 4**

Mushroom and fennel salad

Cook the snow peas in boiling water until just tender, then drain, and toss in the French dressing while still warm. Cool.

Arrange the pepper rings on four plates. Fill each pepper ring with the mushrooms and fennel. Arrange the snow peas on the plates. Blend the mayonnaise with the sour cream, herbs and seasoning. Place a portion of herb mayonnaise in the center of each plate. **Serves 4**

Italian salad

Put the wine, water, bay leaves, black peppercorns and lemon peel into a saucepan, and bring to a boil. Set aside for 10 minutes, then strain into a mixing bowl. Add the mushrooms, then chill for at least 1 hour, stirring occasionally.

Cook the beans in boiling water for 3 minutes. Rinse under cold water, and drain. Arrange the salami, beans and chicory on individual plates with the mushrooms in the center. **Serves 4**

Right: Mushroom and fennel salad.

INGREDIENTS

1½ cups cracked wheat (bulgur)
1¼ cups red wine
⅔ cup water
1 pound medium button mushrooms
vinaigrette dressing
2 apples
lemon juice
6 ounces herbed cheese

½ pound snow peas, strings removed
2 tablespoons French dressing
1 each green, yellow and red bell pepper, seeded and cut into rings
½ pound medium button mushrooms, sliced
½ cup diced Italian fennel
3 tablespoons mayonnaise
3 tablespoons sour cream
4 tablespoons chopped parsley
2 tablespoons chopped fresh tarragon
2 tablespoons snipped fresh chives

6 tablespoons white wine
2 tablespoons water
3 bay leaves
1 teaspoon black peppercorns
strip of lemon peel
1 pound small button mushrooms
¼ pound small stringless green beans
¼ pound salami, sliced
chicory or crisp lettuce, shredded

Summer salad

Peel the garlic, slice, and crush it with salt on a board with a chef knife until it is smooth and creamy. Mix together the garlic, vinegar, oil and pepper, and marinate the mushrooms in the sauce for several hours or overnight.

Halve the avocados, and remove the pits and peel. Slice the avocados, and toss in lemon juice. Arrange the avocado and chicory on plates with the marinated mushrooms. **Serves 4**

Mushroom and celeriac salad

To make the sauce, mix the mayonnaise with the sour cream and seasoning. (For a less rich sauce, replace the sour cream with the same quantity of natural yogurt.) Fold in the mushrooms, celeriac and carrot. Chill before serving, garnished with chopped parsley. **Serves 4-6**

Tossed mushroom and walnut salad

Cook the green beans in boiling water for 2 minutes. Rinse with cold water, then drain well. Sprinkle the pears with a little lemon juice. Mix the walnuts, mushrooms, lettuce, green beans and pears in a salad bowl. Whisk together the ingredients for the dressing, pour over salad, and then toss. Garnish with enoki mushrooms. **Serves 4**

Top right: Summer salad; Tossed mushroom and walnut salad (center left); Mushroom and celeriac salad (bottom).

INGREDIENTS

2 cloves garlic
4 tablespoons red wine vinegar
6 tablespoons sunflower oil
1 pound brown mushrooms
2 avocados
lemon juice
chicory

¾ pound small button mushrooms, halved
½ large celeriac root, peeled and coarsely grated
1½ cups coarsely grated carrot
SAUCE
¾ cup mayonnaise made with white wine vinegar
⅔ cup sour cream
GARNISH
chopped parsley

¼ pound small green beans, strings removed
2 ripe pears, peeled, cored and roughly chopped
lemon juice
1 cup walnut halves
1 pound small button mushrooms
1 head leaf lettuce, torn into small pieces
DRESSING
3 tablespoons sesame oil
3 tablespoons cider vinegar
2 teaspoons dark brown sugar
GARNISH
¼ pound enoki mushrooms

Warm mushroom and turkey liver salad

Arrange the chicory on individual plates. Heat 1 tablespoon of the oil in a skillet, and brown the pine nuts, then remove. Heat the remaining oil, and cook the turkey livers over a medium heat for about 3 minutes. Add the mushrooms, and cook for a further 3 minutes, stirring occasionally. Remove the turkey livers, and slice quickly (the inside should still be pink). Add the vinegar and seasoning to the skillet with the pine nuts and turkey livers. Heat through, then serve on top of the chicory. **Serves 4-6**

Mushroom and seafood salad

Pour the wine over the mushrooms. Add the thyme and seasoning, and mix well. Cover, and chill for 2 hours. Mix the remaining ingredients together. Stir in the mushrooms with any juices, and toss together. **Serves 4**

Chicken salad

Put the oil, vinegar, marjoram and seasoning into a saucepan. Bring to a boil, then pour into a mixing bowl with the mushrooms. Mix well, then leave until cold, stirring occasionally.

Wash and drain the chicory or lettuce, then tear into small pieces. Toss with the chicken, grapes and radishes. Arrange the salad around the edge of a serving platter, then pile the mushroom mixture in the center. **Serves 4**

Top: Chicken salad; Warm mushroom and turkey liver salad (center); Mushroom and seafood salad (bottom).

INGREDIENTS

½ small head chicory
2 tablespoons oil
¼ cup pine nuts
½ pound turkey livers
½ pound brown mushrooms, quartered
2 tablespoons red wine vinegar

❧

5 tablespoons white wine
¾ pound small button mushrooms
2 teaspoons chopped fresh thyme
6 ounces bean sprouts, blanched in boiling water for 15 seconds, then drained
6 ounces peeled cooked shrimp
¼ pound crab sticks, each cut into 3
1 small cucumber, sliced

❧

2 tablespoons olive oil
4 tablespoons red wine vinegar
2 teaspoons chopped fresh marjoram
1 pound small or medium button mushrooms
chicory or crisp lettuce leaves
1½ cups diced cooked chicken
6 ounces grapes, halved and seeds removed
8 large radishes, halved and sliced

Mushroom, ham and pasta salad

Cook the pasta according to the instructions on the package. Drain, and cool. Mix the pasta, cucumber, ham, mushrooms and tomatoes together. Whisk the remaining ingredients together, then pour the dressing onto the pasta and mix well. Chill for 3-4 hours before serving so that the mushroom mixture is marinated in the dressing. Stir the salad gently after 2 hours and again just before serving. **Serves 4**

Spinach, mushroom and bacon salad

Pick over the spinach very carefully, and remove all the stalks and any large tough leaves. Wash in cold water, and drain well. Broil the bacon until it is really crisp. Leave to cool, then cut into small pieces.

Arrange the spinach in a large salad bowl. Halve the avocado and remove the pit and peel. Slice the avocado thinly, and toss in lemon juice. Arrange the avocado slices on the spinach. Add the mushrooms and sprinkle with the bacon and chives or scallions.

Mix all the dressing ingredients in a jar with a lid and shake well. Just before serving pour over the salad. Garnish with enoki mushrooms. **Serves 4**

Top right: Mushroom, ham and pasta salad; Spinach, mushroom and bacon salad (bottom left).

INGREDIENTS

½ pound pasta spirals
½ cucumber, cut into thin matchsticks
¼ pound piece of cooked ham, cubed
¾ pound small button mushrooms
½ pound tomatoes, peeled, seeded, then chopped
2 tablespoons oil
1 tablespoon vinegar
1 tablespoon chopped fresh oregano

❧

½ pound fresh small-leaf spinach
8 slices bacon
1 avocado
juice of ½ lemon
1 pound small button mushrooms
1 tablespoon snipped fresh chives or chopped scallions
DRESSING
4 tablespoons olive or salad oil
1 tablespoon dry sherry
1 tablespoon lemon juice
grated lemon peel
pinch of superfine sugar
pinch of dry mustard
GARNISH
enoki mushrooms

Main Meals

Mushrooms make a meal. Serve them as a vegetable, broiled or poached, or add them to your favorite recipes. The paler, medium button mushrooms are best with fish and chicken whilst the more mature large white mushrooms complement red meats. Mushrooms are also marvelous in stir-fries. They hold their shape and enjoy being cooked quickly over a high heat.

Zucchini and mushroom fettucini

Heat the oil, and cook the zucchini, onion, garlic, and mushrooms in a covered saucepan over a low heat for a few minutes. Stir in the tomatoes, herbs, turmeric, and sherry. Bring to a boil, and simmer gently for 5 minutes. Add the cream and seasoning, and simmer for a further 20 minutes.

Meanwhile, cook the fettucini according to the instructions on the package. Serve the zucchini and mushroom mixture on top of the fettucini. **Serves 4**

Sauté of pork in cider

Heat the oil in a wok or large skillet, add the beans, cover, and cook for about 3 minutes. Add the pork and onion, and cook for 3 minutes. Stir in the mushrooms, and cook for 1 minute. Stir in the cider, sage, olives and seasoning. Cook for about 5 minutes. Blend the cornstarch with a little water, then stir into the pork mixture. Bring to a boil, then serve on a bed of rice. **Serves 4**

Right: Zucchini and mushroom fettucini.

INGREDIENTS

2 tablespoons oil
¾ pound zucchini, sliced
1 onion, sliced
2 cloves garlic, crushed
¾ pound medium button mushrooms, sliced
8-ounce can peeled chopped tomatoes
½ teaspoon dried basil
½ teaspoon dried mint
1 teaspoon turmeric
5 tablespoons sherry
⅔ cup heavy cream
½ pound fettucini

2 tablespoons oil
6 ounces small stringless green beans, cut into 2-inch lengths
1 pound pork tenderloin, cut into narrow strips
1 large onion, cut into narrow wedge-shaped strips
¾ pound large white mushrooms, sliced
4 tablespoons medium-dry hard cider
1 tablespoon chopped fresh sage
12 pimento-stuffed olives
2 teaspoons cornstarch

Steak and mushroom pie

Cut the steak into 1-inch cubes, and coat in the seasoned flour. Put half the steak into a 1½-quart casserole dish. Add the onion, mushrooms and herbs, then fill the casserole with the remaining steak, but do not pack it tightly. Pour in enough stock to three-quarter fill the casserole.

Roll the dough about ⅛ inch thick, and use to cover the casserole. Brush with beaten egg. Bake in a preheated 425°F oven for 30 minutes; then reduce the oven temperature to 375°F, cover the pie with a sheet of wet waxed paper, and continue cooking for at least 1¼ hours until the steak is tender. Check by inserting a skewer through the pie crust into the steak. **Serves 4**

Chicken and mushroom pie

To make the pie crust dough, cut the margarine into the flour and salt until the mixture resembles fine breadcrumbs. Add enough cold water to make a stiff dough. Cover, and chill.

To make the filling, cut the skinned and boneless chicken breast halves into large pieces, and coat in the flour. Put into a 1½-quart casserole dish with the mushrooms, carrots and red pepper. Mix together the chicken stock, lemon peel, lemon juice and black pepper. Pour over the chicken.

Roll out the dough, and use to cover the casserole. Make two slits in the center of the pie crust. Use the dough trimmings to make leaves. Arrange on top of the pie, and brush with a little milk. Bake in a preheated 425°F oven for 15 minutes; then reduce the oven temperature to 375°F, and cook for a further 40 minutes. **Serves 6**

Top left: Steak and mushroom pie; Chicken and mushroom pie (bottom right).

INGREDIENTS

1¼ pounds chuck steak
3 tablespoons all-purpose flour, seasoned
1 onion, sliced
1 pound large white mushrooms
½ teaspoon mixed dried herbs
about 1½ cups beef stock
rich flaky pastry dough for pie crust
beaten egg, to glaze

❧

PIE CRUST DOUGH
½ cup margarine
1¾ cups all-purpose flour
pinch of salt
FILLING
6 skinned and boneless chicken breast halves
5 tablespoons all-purpose flour
1 pound medium button mushrooms, sliced
4 carrots, sliced
1 red bell pepper, seeded and chopped
1¼ cups chicken stock
grated peel of 1 lemon
1 tablespoon lemon juice
black pepper
milk, to glaze

❧

Honey-glazed pork and mushrooms

This recipe is ideal for people with limited cooking facilities – for example, in a vacation home or on a boat.

Put the chops in a non-stick skillet, and cook over a low heat for about 2 minutes on each side. Stir in the honey, mustard and mushrooms. Cover, and cook gently for 8-10 minutes, turning the chops over halfway through the cooking time. Serve sprinkled with parsley. **Serves 2**

Lamb with mushroom and orange sauce

Mix the ingredients for the marinade together, then pour over the chops. Cover, and chill for at least 4 hours, turning the chops over occasionally. Remove the chops from the marinade, reserving the juices.

To make the sauce, heat the oil, and cook the onion and garlic until soft. Stir in the mushrooms, and cook for a further 3 minutes. Pour the orange juice into a measuring cup with the reserved marinade, then make up to 2 cups with water. Pour over the mushrooms, and bring to a boil. Cover the pan, and simmer gently for about 10 minutes.

Meanwhile cook the chops under a preheated broiler for 6-8 minutes on each side.

Blend the cornstarch with a little water until smooth, then stir into the mushroom mixture. Bring to a boil, stirring continuously, then season the sauce to taste. Serve with the chops. Note: This sauce is equally delicious served with duck. **Serves 4**

Top right: Honey-glazed pork and mushrooms; Lamb with mushroom and orange sauce (bottom left).

INGREDIENTS

2 pork loin chops
2 tablespoons honey
2 teaspoons whole-grain mustard
5 ounces small button mushrooms
GARNISH
chopped parsley

❧

4-6 lamb loin chops
MARINADE
juice of 1 large orange
4 teaspoons chopped fresh mint
2 teaspoons cider vinegar
2 teaspoons olive oil
SAUCE
2 tablespoons oil
1 small onion, finely chopped
2 cloves garlic, crushed
½ pound brown mushrooms, sliced
juice of 2 oranges
4-5 teaspoons cornstarch

❧

Stir-fried chicken, mushrooms and shrimp

Heat the oil in a wok or large skillet, then stir in the celery and onion. Cover, and cook over a low heat for 3 minutes. Stir in the garlic, mushrooms, chicken, shrimp, and seasoning. Cover, and continue cooking for 8-10 minutes, stirring occasionally. Stir in the lemon juice. Serve garnished with parsley and lemon slices. **Serves 4**

Stir-fried chili beef

Add water to the orange juice to make 1 cup. Put the steak in a mixing bowl with the diluted orange juice, chilies and lemon juice. Mix well, cover, and leave to marinate for at least 1 hour. Drain the steak, reserving the juices.

Heat the oil in a wok or large skillet, and stir in the steak and onion. Cover, and cook for 3 minutes. Stir in the beans, red pepper and mushrooms. Cover, and cook for 3 minutes. Stir in the reserved marinade. Bring to a boil, then stir in the peanut butter and seasoning, and cook until the sauce thickens. Serve garnished with fresh herbs. **Serves 4**

Spicy stir-fried kidneys

Make crisscross cuts in a lattice pattern halfway through the thickness of each kidney. Heat the oil in a wok or large skillet. Stir in the kidneys and potatoes, cover, and cook for 5 minutes. Stir in the carrots and zucchini, cover, and cook for 5 minutes. Stir in the remaining ingredients, cover, and cook for 20 minutes, stirring occasionally. **Serves 4**

Right: Stir-fried chili beef.

INGREDIENTS

2 tablespoons oil
3 stalks celery, finely chopped
1 large onion, sliced lengthwise
2 cloves garlic, crushed
¾ pound large white mushrooms
10 ounces chicken breast fillets, cut into strips
¼ pound peeled cooked shrimp
2 tablespoons lemon juice

juice of 2 oranges
1¼ pounds beef round or sirloin steak, cut into thin strips
1-2 dried red chilies, crushed
2 tablespoons lemon juice
2 tablespoons oil
1 large onion, sliced into wedges
6 ounces fresh fava beans or lima beans
1 red bell pepper, seeded and cut into thin strips
¾ pound medium button mushrooms, thickly sliced
4 tablespoons peanut butter

5-6 lambs' kidneys, halved and cored
2 tablespoons oil
¾ pound small new potatoes, quartered
6 ounces new carrots, thinly sliced
½ pound zucchini, thinly sliced
½ pound brown mushrooms, sliced
¼-½ teaspoon hot chili powder
1 teaspoon turmeric
1 teaspoon ground coriander
4 tablespoons water

Fish crumble

Remove the skin from the smoked cod fillet and cut the fish into large cubes.

Heat the oil, and cook the leeks and carrots for 2 minutes. Add the mushrooms, and cook for 2 minutes. Stir in the flour, and cook for a minute. Remove from the heat, and stir in the milk gradually. Return to the heat, and bring to a boil, stirring. Stir in three-quarters of the cheese, and set aside.

Arrange the fish in a 1-quart ovenproof dish, then cover with the sauce. Rub the butter into the rolled oats, stir in the remaining cheese, then sprinkle over the fish and sauce. Bake in a preheated 375°F oven for about 30 minutes. **Serves 4**

Mushroom-stuffed chicken

Melt the butter, and cook the onion and mushrooms for 3 minutes. Stir in the garlic, and cook for 30 seconds. Turn into a mixing bowl with the lime peel and juice, rice and seasoning. Leave to cool.

Meanwhile, wipe the chicken all over with paper towels. Then, beginning at the neck end, insert your hands very carefully between the skin and the breast of the bird, and ease the skin away from the breast slowly.

Use about three-quarters of the stuffing to form an even layer between the skin and the flesh of the chicken. Use the remainder to fill the neck end. Secure the neck flap with skewers or twine. Weigh the stuffed chicken, and calculate the cooking time. Brush the chicken lightly with oil, and season. Put into a roasting pan, and bake in a preheated 375°F oven for 20 minutes per pound plus 20 minutes. If the stuffing seems to be overbrowning, cover the chicken with wet waxed paper. **Serves 4-6**

Right: Mushroom-stuffed chicken.

INGREDIENTS

1 pound smoked cod fillet
2 tablespoons oil
6 ounces leeks, sliced
2 carrots, diced
¾ pound medium button mushrooms, thickly sliced
3 tablespoons all-purpose flour
1 cup milk
1 cup grated Cheddar cheese
2 tablespoons butter
⅓ cup regular rolled oats

❦

3½-pound roasting chicken
oil
STUFFING
2 tablespoons butter
1 small onion, finely chopped
6 ounces medium button mushrooms, very finely chopped
1 clove garlic, crushed
grated peel and juice of ½ lime
⅓ cup Basmati rice, cooked and drained

NOTE
The stuffing ingredients can be doubled to stuff a 10-pound turkey

Light Meals

One of the best ways to make a quick meal is with mushrooms. Mushrooms on toast, stuffed mushrooms or toasted bacon and mushroom sandwiches are all firm favorites. Make a pasta sauce or a pizza more interesting with sliced mushrooms. These recipes are ideal for people with limited cooking facilities in, say, a vacation cottage or small apartment.

Mushrooms with pasta quills

Put the mushrooms, scallions and thyme into a large mixing bowl, and pour over the grape juice. Mix well, cover, and chill for about 3 hours, stirring occasionally. Stir in the grapes and cooled pasta just before serving. **Serves 4**

Tagliatelle with mushrooms and garlic cheese

Heat the oil and butter together in a saucepan, add the mushrooms and garlic, cover, and cook gently for about 5 minutes. Stir in the spinach, and cook for a minute. Stir in the ricotta, white wine and seasoning, and cook gently for about 3 minutes. Add the tagliatelle carefully, and fold the sauce through the pasta. Serve immediately, garnished with parsley. **Serves 4**

Right: Mushrooms with pasta quills.

INGREDIENTS

¾ pound small button mushrooms
6 large scallions, chopped
1 tablespoon chopped fresh thyme
¾ cup white or purple grape juice
½ pound white seedless grapes, halved
6 ounces pasta quills, cooked and drained

2 tablespoons oil
1 tablespoon butter
¾ pound small button mushrooms, halved
2 cloves garlic, crushed
½ pound frozen chopped spinach, thawed and drained
½ pound ricotta cheese
5 tablespoons white wine
½ pound fresh tagliatelle, cooked and drained

Mushrooms on toast

Trim the mushroom stalks (use for soup or stock). Preheat the broiler. Melt the butter in a saucepan (or in a microwave). Put the mushrooms, cap side up, on a wire rack, and brush with half the butter. Broil for 2 minutes. Turn the mushrooms over. Brush with the remaining butter, and broil for a further 2 minutes. Serve on toast. If desired, season with black pepper, lemon juice, Worcestershire sauce or sherry. (Alternatively, cook in a microwave on High for 2 minutes.) **Serves 2**

Toasted bacon and mushroom sandwich

Preheat a sandwich toaster. Oil a skillet lightly, add the bacon, and cook gently for 3 minutes until the fat begins to run. Add the mushrooms, and cook briskly until the bacon is crisp. Season with black pepper. If desired, add the beaten egg, and cook for 1 minute. Butter the bread on one side only. Place two slices of the bread in the toaster, butter side down, and spoon the mushroom mixture on top. Cover with the remaining slices of bread, butter side up, and cook until brown. **Makes 2 sandwiches**

Deviled mushrooms

Mix the fromage frais, Worcestershire sauce and mustard together in a saucepan. Stir in the mushrooms, and cook over a low heat for about 6 minutes. Do not allow the mixture to boil. Serve with triangles of toast. **Serves 4**

Top left: Toasted bacon and mushroom sandwich; Deviled mushrooms (top right); Mushrooms on toast (bottom).

INGREDIENTS

½ pound large white mushrooms
2 tablespoons butter
2 slices toast
black pepper (optional)
lemon juice (optional)
Worcestershire sauce or sherry (optional)

❧

1 teaspoon oil
2 slices bacon, chopped
¼ pound large white mushrooms, sliced
black pepper
butter
4 slices bread
1 beaten egg (optional)

❧

⅔ cup very low-fat natural fromage frais
2 teaspoons Worcestershire sauce
2 teaspoons whole-grain mustard
½ pound large white mushrooms, sliced
TO SERVE
triangles of toast

❧

Stuffed mushrooms

Melt half the butter in a saucepan, and cook the minced chicken and onion for about 5 minutes, stirring occasionally. Leave to cool, then stir in the breadcrumbs, herbs and seasoning. Mix well, and divide among the mushrooms. Arrange the mushrooms in a roasting pan and dot with the remaining butter. Bake in a preheated 375°F oven for 20-25 minutes. **Serves 2**

Souffléd omelet

To make the filling, heat the oil, and cook the mushrooms gently for about 4 minutes, stirring occasionally. Stir in the flour and paprika, and cook for a minute. Add the remaining ingredients gradually, and bring to a boil, stirring continuously, then cook over a very low heat while making the omelet.

   Beat the egg yolks, milk and thyme together. Whisk the egg whites, then fold into the yolk mixture. Make the omelet as usual, then place the pan under a preheated broiler, and cook until golden. Slide the omelet onto a plate. Spoon the filling onto one half of the omelet, then flip over. **Serves 1**

Mushroom gnocchi

Melt 2 tablespoons of the butter, and fry the mushrooms for 3 minutes. Drain, then beat in the cheeses, beaten egg, flour, nutmeg and seasoning. Leave until cold. With well-floured hands, shape large spoonfuls of the mixture into balls. Lower into a large pan of simmering water, and cook for 4 minutes. Drain. Keep hot in a warm oven. Sauté the garlic in the remaining butter for 30 seconds. Pour over the gnocchi, and sprinkle with parsley. **Serves 4**

Right: Stuffed mushrooms.

INGREDIENTS

¼ cup butter
⅔ cup minced chicken breast fillet
1 small onion, minced
⅓ cup fresh whole-wheat breadcrumbs
1 tablespoon chopped, mixed fresh herbs
4 large white mushrooms

2 eggs, separated
1 tablespoon milk
1 teaspoon chopped fresh thyme
FILLING
1 tablespoon oil
¼ pound brown mushrooms, sliced
1 teaspoon all-purpose flour
½ teaspoon paprika
3 tablespoons milk
1 teaspoon tomato paste

⅓ cup butter
¾ pound medium button mushrooms, very finely chopped
½ pound low-fat soft cheese
⅓ cup grated Parmesan cheese
2 eggs, beaten
5 tablespoons all-purpose flour
freshly grated nutmeg
1 large clove garlic, crushed
GARNISH
chopped parsley

Mushroom pizza

Make up the pizza crust according to the instructions on the package, using ½ cup hot water and 2 tablespoons oil. Roll the dough to a 12-inch circle, and put on a greased baking sheet. Heat the remaining oil in a large skillet, and stir-fry the mushrooms quickly for 1 minute. Add the garlic and basil, and stir-fry for a further minute. Spoon the mushrooms over the pizza crust, season, and sprinkle the grated mozzarella on top. Bake in a preheated 425°F oven for 20 minutes. **Serves 2**

Mushrooms in garlic butter

Fry the mushrooms lightly in hot oil for about 20 seconds, then drain well on paper towels. Mix the butter, garlic, herbs, seasoning and lemon juice together. Arrange the mushrooms, stalk side uppermost, in a shallow baking pan. Spoon a little of the garlic butter into each mushroom, then press some breadcrumbs lightly on top. Cook under a medium broiler for about 5 minutes until the breadcrumbs are golden-brown. Serve on small heated plates. Pour over any remaining melted garlic butter, and serve with crusty bread. **Serves 4**

Top right: Mushroom pizza; Mushrooms in garlic butter (bottom).

INGREDIENTS

6.5-ounce package pizza crust mix
4 tablespoons oil
¾ pound brown mushrooms, thickly sliced
1 clove garlic, chopped
4 leaves fresh basil, chopped
3 ounces mozzarella cheese, grated

❧

1 pound large white mushrooms
oil for frying
¼ cup unsalted butter, softened
2-3 cloves garlic, crushed
2 tablespoons chopped fresh herbs
2 teaspoons lemon juice
¾ cup fresh breadcrumbs

❧

Mushroom and seafood fried rice

Heat the oil in a large skillet, and cook the onion and celery for about 2 minutes. Stir in the Basmati rice, and cook for a minute, then stir in the curry powder and mushrooms, and cook for a further minute. Stir in the water, and bring to a boil. Simmer gently for 5 minutes. Add the shrimp, mixed peanuts and raisins, and corn, and cook for a further 4 minutes. Stir in the tuna carefully with seasoning to taste, and cook for a minute or until the rice is tender and the water absorbed. Garnish with lemon wedges. **Serves 4**

Smoked cod pie

Heat the oil in a saucepan, and cook the scallions and mushrooms gently. Spoon half into the pastry shell, arrange the fish over the mushrooms, and top with the remaining mushroom mixture. Beat the egg and milk together, and pour over the fish. Bake in a preheated 350°F oven for 40-45 minutes. **Serves 4**

Salami risotto

Heat the oil in a large skillet, and cook the mushrooms and scallions for about 3 minutes. Add the rice and spices, and cook for another minute. Add ⅔ cup of the stock, and simmer gently, stirring occasionally, until the liquid has been absorbed. Add a further ⅔ cup of the stock, and repeat as before. Add the remaining stock and other ingredients. Simmer gently, stirring occasionally, until the stock has been absorbed, and the rice is cooked. **Serves 4**

Right: Mushroom and seafood fried rice.

INGREDIENTS

2 tablespoons oil
1 onion, finely chopped
2 stalks celery, chopped
½ pound Basmati rice
1 tablespoon hot curry powder
¾ pound medium button mushrooms, thickly sliced
2½ cups water
¼ pound frozen peeled cooked shrimp
¼ pound mixed peanuts and raisins
7-ounce can whole-kernel corn, drained
7-ounce can tuna, drained

2 tablespoons oil
⅓ cup scallions, very finely chopped
½ pound medium button mushrooms, thinly sliced
8-inch baked plain pastry shell
6 ounces smoked cod fillet, cooked, skinned and flaked
1 small egg, beaten
6 tablespoons milk

1 tablespoon oil
1 pound medium button mushrooms
1 bunch scallions, chopped
¾ cup risotto rice
1 teaspoon ground turmeric
1 teaspoon ground coriander
2 cups chicken stock
7-ounce can corn with sweet peppers, drained
3 ounces salami, cut into thin strips

Entertaining

Mushrooms grow in a variety of attractive shapes and each has its own special flavor and texture. More cultivated specialty mushrooms are now available, such as oyster and shiitake mushrooms. Buy some of these varieties and mix them with small button mushrooms. Here are some exotic recipes to impress your guests.

Sauté of specialty mushrooms

To make the spaetzli, put all the ingredients except 2 tablespoons of the oil into a bowl, and beat well. Freeze for 1 hour. Then scrape the dough onto a coarse grater, being careful that the dough forms into large shreds and not lumps. Use a little extra flour if necessary. Plunge the spaetzli into boiling salted water for 1 minute. Drain, and cover with cold water to cool. Strain the spaetzli, and pat dry with paper towels. Heat the remaining olive oil in a large non-stick pan, and sauté the spaetzli until golden-brown. Drain on paper towels and keep warm.

Trim the stalks from the mushrooms and put into a saucepan with ⅔ cup water. Bring to a boil, and simmer for a few minutes. Strain off the liquid, and use for mushroom stock.

Heat the oil in the large non-stick pan until very hot. Sauté the mushrooms for 1 minute. Add the shallots, and continue to sauté. Pour in the liqueur, add the mushroom stock, and cook until the quantity of liquid is reduced by half; then add the veal stock, and again cook until the quantity of liquid is reduced by half. Stir in the herbs and butter. Season to taste. Add the spaetzli, and serve immediately with the arugula salad. **Serves 4**

Right: Sauté of specialty mushrooms.

INGREDIENTS

SPAETZLI
1¼ cups all-purpose flour
2 small eggs
¼ teaspoon grated nutmeg
3 tablespoons olive oil

SAUTE
1½ pounds mixed small button, oyster and shiitake mushrooms
4 teaspoons olive oil
4 shallots, finely chopped
1 tablespoon frangelico or amaretto liqueur
⅔ cup mushroom stock (see method)
⅔ cup veal or chicken stock
1 tablespoon chopped fresh chervil
1 tablespoon chopped parsley
2 tablespoons unsalted butter

TO SERVE
arugula salad dressed with balsamico vinaigrette

NOTE
Cooked pasta can be used as an alternative to spaetzli.

Mushroom choux puffs

Melt the margarine slowly in the water. Bring to a boil, then stir in the flour and salt quickly. Beat to a smooth ball. Leave to cool slightly, then beat in the eggs and mustard gradually until smooth and glossy. Stir in the mushrooms. Place 24 spoonfuls of the mixture onto a lightly greased baking sheet. Bake in a pre-heated 400°F oven for 15 minutes, then reduce the oven temperature to 350°F, and cook for a further 15-20 minutes. Serve hot, using toothpicks. **Makes 24**

Golden mushroom and cod nuggets

Blend the sour cream and horseradish sauce together, then chill. Put the cod and mushrooms into a food processor, and blend until fairly smooth. Add the parsley and seasoning. Shape into 24 balls, then chill for at least 1 hour.

Mix the breadcrumbs and hazelnuts together. Dip the balls into the egg, then coat in the breadcrumb mixture. Chill until ready to fry in hot oil until golden-brown. Drain, then serve hot with the horseradish sauce. Garnish with cilantro. **Makes 24**

Mushroom dip with crudités

Put all the ingredients into a food processor and blend until fairly smooth. Turn into a serving dish. Cover, and chill for about 1 hour. Serve surrounded by salad vegetables. **Serves 10**

Top, center: Mushroom dip with crudités; Golden mushroom and cod nuggets (left); Mushroom choux puffs (bottom, right).

INGREDIENTS

¼ cup margarine
½ cup water
7 tablespoons bread flour
pinch of salt
2 small eggs, beaten
1-2 teaspoons Dijon mustard
¼ pound brown mushrooms, roughly chopped

⅔ cup sour cream
2 tablespoons horseradish sauce
½ pound cod fillet, skinned and chopped
½ pound medium button mushrooms, chopped
3 tablespoons chopped parsley
1 cup whole-wheat breadcrumbs
4 tablespoons chopped hazelnuts
1 egg, beaten
oil for deep frying
GARNISH
cilantro

2 stalks celery, very finely chopped
½ pound small button mushrooms, very finely chopped
¼ pound low-fat fromage frais, flavored with garlic and parsley
4 tablespoons plain yogurt
TO SERVE
a selection of fresh salad vegetables

Stilton and mushroom vol-au-vent

Cook the vol-au-vent cases according to the instructions on the package. Meanwhile, heat the oil, and cook the celery and mushrooms for 3 minutes. Stir in the flour, and cook for a minute. Stir in the milk gradually, and bring to a boil, stirring continuously. Add the apple, and cook for a minute. Add the Stilton and seasoning, stirring until the cheese has melted. Fill the vol-au-vent cases with the sauce and serve. **Makes 16**

Duck and mushroom special

Prepare the mushrooms by making a series of curved cuts with a sharp knife from the top of the mushroom to the bottom edge. Remove a narrow strip along each cut.

Discard the excess fat from the duck breasts. Heat the oil, then cook the duck, skin side up, over a high heat until just browned. Transfer to a wire rack placed in a roasting pan. Cook the duck in a preheated 450°F oven for 6-8 minutes, then transfer to a warmed plate, and set aside.

Heat the oil remaining in the roasting pan, and cook the mushrooms and peppercorns for about 3 minutes. Remove the mushrooms with a slotted spoon, and keep warm. Stir in the flour, and cook for 1 minute. Stir in the cognac, stock and seasoning gradually. Bring to a boil, stirring, and reduce the quantity by half. Then stir in the cream gradually; do not allow it to boil as it could then curdle.

Remove the skin from the duck breasts quickly, and discard. Slice the duck thinly, then re-shape into breasts. Spoon the sauce onto warmed plates. Arrange the duck and mushrooms on the sauce. Garnish with cilantro. **Serves 2**

Right: Duck and mushroom special.

INGREDIENTS

16 frozen individual vol-au-vent cases
3 tablespoons oil
1 stalk celery, finely chopped
½ pound small button mushrooms, sliced
3 tablespoons all-purpose flour
3 cups milk
1 apple, peeled, cored and diced
1½ cups grated Stilton cheese

❧

10 ounces medium button mushrooms, stalks trimmed
2 large duck breasts
1 tablespoon oil
1½ tablespoons green peppercorns in vinegar, drained
2 teaspoons all-purpose flour
5 tablespoons cognac
scant 1 cup chicken stock
5 tablespoons light cream
GARNISH
sprig of cilantro

Golden mushroom and tomato pie

Place a 10-inch fluted flan pan with a removable bottom on a baking sheet. Brush with a little butter. Unfold the pastry, brush one sheet with butter, fold in half, and place in the pie pan so that it extends over the sides. Brush the top with butter. Repeat with 5 more sheets, placing them in the pie pan so that the corners project like the spokes of a wheel.

Arrange the mushrooms, tomatoes, thyme and cheese in layers on top of pastry. Bring the pastry edges over toward the center. Brush the remaining sheets of pastry with butter, fold in half, then place on top of the pie, tucking down the edges. Brush the top with butter. Bake in a preheated 375°F oven for about 25 minutes until crisp and golden-brown. **Serves 4**

Mille feuille of mushrooms

Thaw the puff pastry according to the instructions on the package. Cut into four triangles. Score a smaller triangle within each triangle. Brush with egg wash, and bake in a preheated 400°F oven for 10 minutes. Meanwhile, heat the calvados in a large shallow pan. Add the mushrooms, and flambé. Remove the mushrooms, and keep warm. Boil the remaining calvados until reduced by half, and reserve. In a separate pan, cook the shallot, garlic and bacon for 3 minutes. Add the mustard, cream, pepper and reserved calvados. Heat gently, but do not boil. Stir in the butter in small pieces to thicken the sauce.

Remove the inner triangle from each pastry case carefully, fill with the cooked mushrooms, and pour a little sauce over them. Replace the "lids." Pour the remaining sauce around the pastry cases. Garnish with fried apple slices. **Makes 4**

Right: Golden mushroom and tomato pie.

INGREDIENTS

scant ⅓ cup butter, melted
8 sheets filo pastry
¾ pound medium button mushrooms, sliced
2 beefsteak tomatoes, peeled, seeded and chopped
2 teaspoons chopped fresh thyme
1½ cups grated Cheddar cheese

8-inch square sheet frozen puff pastry (or roll puff pastry to make 8-inch square, ¼ inch thick)
beaten egg and milk
⅔ cup calvados
¾ pound mixed small button, oyster and shiitake mushrooms
1 shallot, finely chopped
1 clove garlic, finely chopped
1 slice bacon, finely chopped
1 teaspoon Dijon mustard
⅔ cup heavy cream
pinch of black pepper
2 tablespoons unsalted butter
GARNISH
fried apple slices

Mushroom and salmon molds with lentils

Cook the lentils according to the instructions on the package. Meanwhile, mix together the minced salmon, salt and egg white. Chill. Take half the given quantity of shiitake mushrooms, selecting the larger ones, and cut the mushrooms horizontally across the caps. Heat half the Madeira, and blanch the mushroom slices. Remove with a slotted spoon. Chop the leftover pieces of shiitake mushrooms, discarding the stalks, and blanch in the same Madeira. Boil until the quantity of liquid is reduced by half.

Line four ramekins with the shiitake mushroom slices. Mix ½ cup of the cream into the chilled salmon. Spoon some of the salmon into the ramekins, leaving a well in the center. Add a dash of cream to the chopped cooked shiitake mushrooms, and reduce until thick. Season. Fill the ramekins with the cooked mushrooms, and cover with the remaining salmon mixture. Put the ramekins into a roasting pan filled with hot water, and cook in a preheated 325°F oven for 10-15 minutes.

Meanwhile, pour the stock, wine and the remaining Madeira into a saucepan, and reduce the quantity of liquid by three-quarters. Add the remaining cream, and season to taste. Quarter the remaining shiitake mushrooms, and discard the stalks. Mix with the oyster mushrooms, and poach in the Madeira sauce.

Spoon a pile of cooked lentils onto each plate. Turn out the salmon molds beside the lentils. Pour the Madeira sauce around the salmon, and garnish with asparagus stalks. **Serves 4**

Right: Mushroom and salmon molds with lentils.

INGREDIENTS

½ cup green lentils
½ pound fresh salmon, minced
pinch of salt
1 egg white, lightly beaten
½ pound shiitake or large white mushrooms
scant 1 cup Madeira
scant 1 cup heavy cream
⅔ cup chicken stock
¼ cup white wine
¼ pound oyster mushrooms
GARNISH
cooked asparagus stalks

Vegetarian Recipes

Many of the other recipes in this book are also suitable for vegetarians and vegans, but this chapter is specifically for them. Today, many families or groups have just one vegetarian in their midst and some people find it difficult to cook for them. The recipes will help those non-vegetarians who want to cook a dish that is acceptable to both meat-eaters and vegetarians.

Stir-fried oyster mushrooms

Heat the oil in a wok or large skillet. Stir in the carrots and green pepper, cover, and cook for 1 minute. Stir in the mushrooms, cover, and cook for 2 minutes, stirring occasionally. Add the bamboo shoots, then stir in the remaining ingredients gradually. Bring to a boil, and simmer for 1 minute; then serve garnished with scallion curls. **Serves 4**

Chinese stir-fry

Heat the oil in a wok or large skillet. Stir in the baby corn, red pepper and snow peas. Cover, and cook for 2 minutes. Stir in the scallions, mushrooms and grated ginger, and cook for another minute. Stir in the ground ginger, and cook for a few seconds; then stir in the soy sauce, honey and ketchup. Bring to a boil, cover, and cook gently for about 3 minutes. Stir in the bean sprouts, and cook gently for a further 2 minutes. Blend the cornstarch with a little water until smooth, then stir into the vegetables. Bring to a boil, and serve immediately. **Serves 4**

Right: Chinese stir-fry.

INGREDIENTS

2 tablespoons sesame seed oil
6 ounces carrots, cut into strips
1 green bell pepper, seeded and cubed
½ pound oyster mushrooms, sliced
8-ounce can sliced bamboo shoots, drained
2 tablespoons light soy sauce
2 tablespoons hoisin sauce
2 tablespoons stock

2 tablespoons sesame seed oil
6 baby corn
1 large red bell pepper, seeded and cut into narrow strips
5 ounces snow peas, strings removed
1 bunch scallions, cut into 2-inch lengths
10 ounces small button mushrooms, halved
1-inch piece of ginger root, grated
1 teaspoon ground ginger
4 tablespoons soy sauce
1 tablespoon honey
3 tablespoons ketchup
½ pound fresh bean sprouts
1 tablespoon cornstarch

Mushroom pie

Prick the dough on the bottom of the pie pan very thoroughly with a fork. Then line with a circle of foil or waxed paper, and fill with dried beans. Bake in a preheated 400°F oven for 15 minutes. Remove the beans and foil or paper. Reduce the oven temperature to 375°F.

Meanwhile, heat the margarine and oil in a pan, and fry the onion gently for 2-3 minutes. Do not allow it to brown. Add the mushrooms, parsley and seasoning, and continue to fry gently for about 5 minutes. Beat in the cream and eggs, and pour the mixture into the partially baked pastry case. Continue cooking for 35-40 minutes until the filling is set. Serve with a salad. **Serves 4-6**

Creamy mushroom and parsnip bake

Blend the parsnips in a food processor until smooth. Heat 2 teaspoons of the oil, and brown the onion quickly. Turn into the processor with the parsnips, cilantro, eggs, cream, and seasoning, and blend until fairly smooth. Heat the remaining oil, and cook the mushrooms and cumin seeds for 5 minutes. Drain. Spread the margarine lightly over the bread, and cut each slice into two triangles.

Oil four 1¼-cup ovenproof dishes lightly. Line each dish with four triangles of bread. Spoon in half the parsnip mixture, then half the mushrooms; repeat the layers. Bake in a preheated 375°F oven for about 30 minutes. Serve garnished with sprigs of fresh cilantro. **Serves 4**

Top right: Mushroom pie; Creamy mushroom and parsnip bake (center and bottom).

INGREDIENTS

1 deep 8-inch pie pan with removable
bottom lined with plain pastry dough
2 tablespoons margarine
2 teaspoons oil
1 large onion, sliced
1 pound brown mushrooms, sliced
1 tablespoon chopped parsley
¼ teaspoon garlic salt (optional)
⅔ cup heavy cream
2 small eggs, beaten

❧

1 pound parsnips, cooked and drained
8 teaspoons oil
1 onion, roughly chopped
2 tablespoons chopped fresh cilantro
2 eggs, beaten
3 tablespoons heavy cream
10 ounces large white mushrooms, sliced
1 teaspoon cumin seeds
margarine
8 slices brown bread, crusts removed
GARNISH
sprigs of fresh cilantro

❧

Tossed mixed salad with oranges

Tear the lettuce into small pieces, and put into a salad bowl with the watercress, oranges, green pepper, olives and mushrooms. Mix the avocado with the lemon juice, before spooning into the mushroom mixture, then toss together. **Serves 4**

Layered terrine

To make the carrot layer, melt the margarine, and cook the garlic until soft; then beat into the carrot purée with the thyme, bread-crumbs and egg. Set aside. Mix all the ingredients for the mush-room layer together; then set aside. Pick over the spinach leaves, and discard any thick stalks and yellow leaves. Wash and drain the spinach; then cook in a covered saucepan over a low heat for about 3 minutes. Squeeze out as much moisture as possible, then finely chop the spinach. Melt the margarine in a pan, and cook the onion until soft. Add to the spinach with the egg and a little grated nutmeg.

Oil a 5½-cup terrine lightly. Spoon the carrot mixture into the bottom, and spread evenly. Spoon in the mushroom mixture, then the spinach mixture and spread evenly. Cover with a lightly oiled sheet of foil. Place in a roasting pan half-filled with hot water. Bake in a preheated 325°F oven for about 1 hour 10 minutes, or until the top is firm to the touch. Leave to cool.

Dissolve the gelatin powder in the lemon juice and 2 table-spoons stock in a bowl over a pan of hot water or in a microwave. Make up to 1¼ cups with stock. Pour a very thin layer on top of the spinach. Chill until set. Decorate with sliced mushrooms, then carefully spoon a little more aspic over the top. Chill until set, then carefully spoon a little more aspic over the top. Again chill until set. **Serves 6-8**

Top left: Tossed mixed salad with oranges; Layered terrine (top right and bottom).

INGREDIENTS

1 head leaf lettuce
1 bunch watercress
2 oranges, peeled, halved and sliced
1 green bell pepper, cut into strips
12 pitted ripe olives, halved
½ pound small button mushrooms
2 avocados, peeled, pitted and chopped
2 tablespoons lemon juice

CARROT LAYER
1 tablespoon margarine
2 cloves garlic, crushed
¾ pound carrot, cooked, drained and mashed to a purée
2 teaspoons chopped fresh thyme
⅓ cup fresh whole-wheat breadcrumbs
1 small egg, beaten
MUSHROOM LAYER
½ pound medium button mushrooms, very finely chopped
4 tablespoons sour cream
⅓ cup fresh whole-wheat breadcrumbs
SPINACH LAYER
1 pound fresh spinach
1 tablespoon margarine
1 onion, very finely chopped
1 small egg, beaten
freshly grated nutmeg
ASPIC GLAZE
2 teaspoons unflavored gelatin powder
1 tablespoon lemon juice
vegetable stock (see method)
DECORATION
raw small button mushrooms, sliced

Nutty mushroom and blue cheese pie

Heat the oil, and fry the celery and scallions lightly for about 3 minutes. Stir in the mushrooms, and cook for about 5 minutes. Stir in the flour, and cook for a minute. Remove from the heat, and stir in the water gradually. Return to the heat, and bring to a boil, stirring continuously. Add seasoning and the hazelnuts; then leave to cool.

To make the dough, put the flour and salt into a mixing bowl. Cut in the margarine, and add enough water to form a not too stiff dough. Roll just over half the dough, and use to line a 10-inch flan pan with a removable bottom. Moisten the edges of the dough with water.

Turn the cold mushroom mixture into the flan pan, then sprinkle the cheese over the top. Roll the remaining dough, and use to cover the pie, sealing the edges well. Garnish with leaves cut from the trimmings. Brush with egg or milk, and bake in a preheated 400°F oven for 40 minutes. **Serves 6**

Mushroom and orange nut roast

Heat the oil, and cook the leeks until soft. Turn into a mixing bowl with the remaining ingredients, and mix well. Turn the mixture into a lightly oiled ovenproof dish. Cover with a piece of lightly oiled foil, and bake in a preheated 375°F oven for about 45 minutes. Serve hot or cold, garnished with sliced oranges. **Serves 8**

INGREDIENTS

2 tablespoons vegetable oil
3 stalks celery, chopped
1 bunch scallions, chopped
9 ounces large white mushrooms, thickly sliced
3 tablespoons all-purpose flour
1¼ cups water
3 tablespoons chopped hazelnuts
⅔ cup grated blue cheese
beaten egg or milk
PIE CRUST DOUGH
1 cup all-purpose flour
¾ cup whole-wheat flour
pinch of salt
½ cup margarine

❧

1 tablespoon oil
½ pound leeks, very finely chopped
scant 1 cup very finely chopped pistachios
scant 1 cup very finely chopped hazelnuts
scant 1 cup very finely chopped almonds
grated peel of 1 orange
¾ cup fresh breadcrumbs
½ pound medium button mushrooms, very finely chopped
2 small eggs, beaten
GARNISH
sliced oranges

❧

Top: Nutty mushroom and blue cheese pie; Mushroom and orange nut roast (bottom right, in dish).

Winter mushroom casserole

Heat the oil, and cook the scallions for 2 minutes. Stir in the turnip, carrots, celery and mushrooms, and cook for about 3 minutes. Stir in the flour, and cook for a minute. Remove from the heat, and stir in the tomatoes and stock gradually. Return to the heat, and bring to a boil, stirring. Stir in the remaining ingredients, then simmer gently for about 15 minutes. Garnish with chopped parsley, and serve with chunks of garlic bread. **Serves 4**

Mushroom and ginger ale salad

Mix the mushrooms, melon, tomatoes and scallion together. Add the ginger ale, then cover, and chill for at least 2 hours, stirring occasionally. **Serves 4-6**

Black-eyed pea Bourguignonne

Boil the peas rapidly for 10 minutes, then drain. Heat the oil, and cook the onions quickly until brown. Add the carrots, then cook for 3 minutes. Stir in the peas with the wine, stock, tomato paste and herbs. Bring to a boil, cover, and simmer gently for 50 minutes, adding the mushrooms after 30 minutes. Blend the cornstarch with the water, then stir into the mixture. Boil for 1 minute, then season. **Serves 4**

Right: Black-eyed pea Bourguignonne.

INGREDIENTS

2 tablespoons oil
1 bunch scallions, cut into 2-inch lengths
2 cups diced turnip
2 carrots, diagonally sliced
3 stalks celery, diagonally sliced
¾ pound brown mushrooms
3 tablespoons all-purpose flour
14-ounce can chopped peeled tomatoes
1½ cups vegetable stock
14-ounce can kidney beans, drained
5 teaspoons hot pepper and lime sauce

~

¾ pound button mushrooms, halved
½ Honeydew melon, seeded and cut into balls or cubes
4 tomatoes, peeled, seeded, and cut into strips
1 large scallion, very finely chopped
6 tablespoons ginger ale

~

6 ounces black-eyed peas, soaked overnight and drained
2 tablespoons oil
½ pound pearl onions
½ pound carrots, cut into large chunks
1¼ cups red wine
⅔ cup vegetable stock
2 tablespoons tomato paste
2 bay leaves
2 tablespoons chopped parsley
½ pound small button mushrooms
1 tablespoon cornstarch
1 tablespoon water

Outdoor Eating

*Mushrooms are perfect for barbecues, picnics or lunches on the patio.
Thread onto kebab skewers or wrap in foil to cook on a barbecue.
Vegetarians in particular will love them – so often, a barbecue means
sausages and steaks. If you want to relax on a summer weekend, make a
chilled mousse or pie the day before so you are not tied to the kitchen.*

~~~

Peppered bacon and mushroom kebabs

Boil the potatoes until just tender, then drain and cool quickly to
stop further cooking. Cut the bacon slice in half, and roll up both
pieces. Thread the mushrooms, potatoes, and bacon onto a
kebab skewer. Brush with oil, and keep cool for 1 hour, brushing
with oil again before cooking. Brush with paprika, then with salt.
Cook on a barbecue (or under a preheated broiler) for 5 minutes,
turning once. **Makes 1 kebab**

Pork and apple burgers

Mix all the ingredients together in a bowl. With well-floured
hands, shape the mixture into 8 burgers about 1 inch thick.
Cover, and chill until required. Cook on a barbecue (or under a
preheated broiler) for about 10 minutes on each side, remem-
bering that pork should be thoroughly cooked. **Makes 8 burgers**

Right: Pork and apple burgers.

INGREDIENTS

2 small new potatoes
1 slice bacon
4 medium button mushrooms
oil
paprika
salt

~~~

1¼ pounds ground lean pork
1 small onion, very finely chopped
½ pound large white mushrooms, very
finely chopped
¾ cup fresh whole-wheat breadcrumbs
1½ cups very finely chopped cooking apples
1 small egg, beaten
1 tablespoon prepared mustard

Pickled mushrooms in oil

Pour the vinegar and water into a large enamelled saucepan. Add the cinnamon stick, cloves, peppercorns, bay leaves and salt. Bring to a boil. Add the mushrooms, return to a boil, then boil for 5 minutes. Spread a clean cloth towel on a work surface, and cover with paper towels. Strain the mushrooms, then spread over the paper towels. Do not touch the mushrooms with your hands as they have now been sterilized. Cover lightly with paper towels. Allow the mushrooms to dry out for a few hours.

Spoon some of the mushrooms into sterilized jars without touching with your hands. Pour over enough oil to cover. Continue to add more mushrooms and more oil to fill each jar. Seal tightly, and store in the refrigerator for a month before using. Once opened, eat within a short time. Serve with cold chicken or ham. **Makes about 2 pounds**

Chicken with mushroom and celery stuffing

To make the stuffing, mix all the ingredients together. Stretch each bacon slice over the back of a knife.

Make a large slit down the side of each chicken breast, then gradually enlarge it to make a large pocket in which to insert the stuffing. Wrap a bacon slice around each breast. Mix the glaze ingredients together. Cook the chicken breasts on a barbecue (or under a medium broiler) for 5 minutes, then brush with some of the tomato glaze. Cook for a further 5 minutes. Turn the chicken breasts over, and repeat, brushing with the remaining glaze after 5 minutes. **Serves 4**

Right: Chicken with mushroom and celery stuffing.

INGREDIENTS

2½ cups white wine vinegar
1¼ cups water
1-inch piece of cinnamon stick
2 teaspoons whole cloves
2 teaspoons black peppercorns
2 bay leaves
1 tablespoon salt
2 pounds medium button mushrooms, thickly sliced
1 cup olive oil

4 large slices bacon
4 large boneless chicken breast halves
STUFFING
¼ pound large white mushrooms, very finely chopped
1 stalk celery, very finely chopped
1 small bunch scallions, very finely chopped
2 tablespoons fresh breadcrumbs
2 tablespoons horseradish sauce
TOMATO GLAZE
2 tablespoons ketchup
1 tablespoon soy sauce
1 tablespoon oil

Mushroom packages

To make the filling, put the chickpeas in a food processor, and blend for just 3-4 seconds to chop roughly. Turn into a bowl with the remaining filling ingredients, and mix well. Spoon into the mushrooms, and dot each with a little butter. Wrap the mushrooms individually in buttered foil. Cook the packages on a barbecue for about 8 minutes (or cook, unwrapped, in a pre-heated 400°F oven for about 6 minutes). **Serves 4-6**

Vegetarian Brazil nut burgers

Heat the oil, and cook the leek, zucchini and mushrooms for 5 minutes. Stir in the chili powder, and cook for 30 seconds. Add the remaining ingredients, and mix well. Leave to cool; then shape into about 8 burgers. Cook on a foil tray on a barbecue for about 8 minutes on each side. **Makes about 8 burgers**

Vegetarian kebabs

To make the sauce, heat the oil, and fry the onion and mushrooms for 8 minutes, stirring occasionally. Blend in a food processor for 30 seconds. Add the peanuts, and blend for a further 30 seconds until fairly smooth. Return to the pan with the remaining ingredients. Bring to a boil, then simmer for 10 minutes.

Thread the vegetables onto skewers. Brush with oil and lemon juice. Cook on a barbecue (or under a preheated broiler) for about 10 minutes, turning two or three times, and brushing with oil and lemon juice. Serve with the peanut sauce. **Serves 8**

Top: Mushroom packages; Vegetarian Brazil nut burgers (center); Vegetarian kebabs (front and on plate, with sauce).

INGREDIENTS

8-12 large white mushrooms
¼ cup butter
FILLING
15-ounce can chickpeas, drained
1 bunch scallions, very finely chopped
1 small red bell pepper, seeded and very finely chopped
few drops of hot pepper sauce

1 tablespoon oil
1 leek, very finely chopped
½ pound zucchini, very finely chopped
¾ pound large white mushrooms, very finely chopped
½ teaspoon chili powder
scant 1 cup very finely chopped Brazil nuts
⅓ cup wheat flakes, crushed
1 small egg, beaten

8 baby corn
¼ pound zucchini, cut into 1-inch lengths
1 pound brown mushrooms
8 pearl onions
3 tablespoons oil
3 tablespoons lemon juice
SAUCE
2 tablespoons oil
1 small onion, chopped
½ pound brown mushrooms, chopped
¾ cup unsalted peanuts
⅔ cup water
2 tablespoons soy sauce
few drops of hot pepper sauce

Mushroom crown

Stir the mushrooms, thyme and garlic into the roll mix. Continue as directed on the package to make a soft dough. Knead well for 5 minutes. Divide into 8, and shape into balls. Arrange on a lightly oiled baking sheet in a ring, leaving a small gap between each ball. Cover with oiled plastic wrap. Leave in a warm place for about 35 minutes. Brush the dough with milk, then sprinkle sesame seeds over the top. Bake in a preheated 425°F oven for about 20 minutes. **Makes 8**

Mushroom cheese spread

Melt the butter, and cook the mushrooms for about 5 minutes. Turn into a food processor, and blend until fairly smooth. Add the remaining ingredients, and blend for a further 30 seconds. Turn into a dish, and chill until required. Transport in an insulated cold bag. **Serves 4**

Three-minute mushroom salad

Put all the dressing ingredients into a jar with a lid, and shake well. Pour the dressing over the mushrooms, stir gently until they are well coated. Store in an airtight container in the refrigerator. Transport in an insulated cold bag. **Serves 4**

Top right: Mushroom crown; Pickled mushrooms in oil (in jar; recipe on page 78); Three-minute mushroom salad (center); Mushroom cheese spread (bottom left).

INGREDIENTS

1 pound medium button mushrooms, finely chopped
1 teaspoon chopped fresh thyme
1 large clove garlic, crushed
16-ounce package hot roll mix
milk
sesame seeds

¼ cup unsalted butter
¾ pound medium button mushrooms, chopped
1¼ cups grated Cheddar cheese
2 teaspoons horseradish mustard
2 tablespoons natural yogurt

1 pound small button mushrooms
DRESSING
5 tablespoons olive oil
2 tablespoons red wine vinegar
½ teaspoon mustard powder
1 teaspoon finely chopped fresh herbs
½ teaspoon superfine sugar
salt and pepper

Pickled Mushrooms
in Oil

Chilled mushroom mousse

Melt the butter, and cook the onion and mushrooms for about 3 minutes. Stir in the milk gradually, then leave to cool. Dissolve the gelatin in the water according to the instructions on the package, cool, then whisk into the mushroom mixture. Leave in a cool place until just beginning to set, then beat in the remaining ingredients. Turn into a 1-quart mold. Chill until set. To serve, dip the mold into hot water for a few seconds, then invert onto a serving plate. Garnish with sliced mushrooms and chopped aspic jelly. **Serves 6-8**

Glazed mushroom pie

Spread the bottom of the pastry shell with the whole-grain mustard. Trim the stalks off the mushrooms close to the caps. Reserve about 12 mushrooms. Chop the remaining mushrooms together with the stalks. Heat the oil, and cook the whole mushrooms first. Drain well on paper towels. Cook the remaining chopped mushrooms, and drain well.

    Scatter the chopped mushrooms over the bottom of the pastry shell. Beat the cheese, eggs, parsley and seasoning together, then pour into the pastry shell. Bake in a preheated 350°F oven for 30 minutes. Leave to cool, then arrange the cooked whole mushrooms over the pie. Sprinkle the gelatin over the stock, and stir until the gelatin has dissolved. When the glaze is beginning to set, brush over the mushrooms. Chill until set. **Serves 6-8**

Left: Chilled mushroom mousse; Glazed mushroom pie (right).

INGREDIENTS

2 tablespoons unsalted butter
1 large onion, very finely chopped
¾ pound medium button mushrooms, very finely chopped
1¼ cups milk
1 envelope unflavored gelatin
1 tablespoon water
2 tablespoons creamed horseradish
⅔ cup sour cream
GARNISH
sliced mushrooms
chopped aspic jelly

1 baked 10-inch pastry shell
1 tablespoon whole-grain mustard
¾ pound large white mushrooms
4 tablespoons oil
¾ pound cottage cheese
2 medium eggs, beaten
1 tablespoon chopped parsley
2 teaspoons unflavored gelatin powder
generous ¾ cup very hot clear vegetable stock

Microwave Recipes

All the recipes in this chapter have been cooked in a 650-watt microwave with turntable and variable power. Mushrooms cook particularly well in a microwave. It takes just 2 minutes to cook ½ pound mushrooms on High. If cooked in a little stock, this quantity accounts for only 68 calories. Mushrooms also taste delicious cooked in a little garlic butter.

Chilled mushrooms

Put the oil, wine, bay leaves, coriander seeds and grated peel from the oranges into a 2-quart glass bowl. Cook, uncovered, on High for 3 minutes. Add the mushrooms, and cover with a glass plate. Cook on Medium for 3 minutes. Remove from the microwave, stir with a wooden spoon, return to the microwave, and cook on Medium for a further 3 minutes. Transfer the mushrooms to another bowl, using a slotted spoon. Strain the cooking liquor, season, and pour over the mushrooms. Remove the pith from the oranges, and cut the flesh into slices. Stir into the mushrooms, cover, cool, then chill for 6 hours. **Serves 8**

Warm mushroom salad

Spin or pat the spinach dry, then shred into a large bowl. Add the onion, red pepper and toasted cubes, and mix well. Put the oil and garlic into a large glass dish. Cover, and cook on High for 45 seconds. Stir in the remaining ingredients. Cover, and cook on High for 3 minutes, stirring halfway through the cooking. Stir the mushroom mixture into the spinach. Cover, and cook on High for 1½ minutes. Toss, and serve. **Serves 4-6**

Right: Warm mushroom salad.

INGREDIENTS

3 tablespoons vegetable oil
⅔ cup white wine
2 bay leaves
8 coriander seeds
2 small (or 1 large) oranges
1½ pounds small button mushrooms
GARNISH
sprig of parsley

¾ pound fresh spinach, tough stalks and yellow leaves discarded, washed
1 onion, thinly sliced
1 red bell pepper, seeded and finely sliced
3 slices granary bread, toasted and cut into cubes
3 tablespoons olive oil
2 cloves garlic, crushed
3 tablespoons lemon juice
1 pound medium button mushrooms, sliced

Baked potatoes

Prick the potatoes all over with a fork, then cook on High for 20 minutes. Meanwhile, pour the oil into a large glass bowl, add the garlic and mushrooms, and stir gently to coat the mushrooms. Stir in the bacon and chives. Cover. Remove the cooked potatoes from the microwave, and wrap each one in foil. Set aside. Cook the mushrooms and bacon on High for 5 minutes. Stir, then cook on High for a further 2 minutes. Slit the potato skins, and scoop out the centers. Mash the potato, and mix with the mushrooms and bacon, together with their juices. Season to taste. Fill the potatoes with the mixture, and serve with a green salad. **Serves 4**

Mushroom scramble

Put the mushrooms in a large glass dish. Add 1 teaspoon water. Cover, and cook on High for 2 minutes. Meanwhile, beat together the eggs, milk and seasoning in a glass cup. Add the butter. Cook on High for 2½-3 minutes, stirring once. Arrange the mushrooms, cap side down, on the toast, and spoon the scrambled egg on top. Serve immediately. (The ingredients can be increased to serve more people. However, scrambled eggs are best cooked in small quantities, and eaten at once.) **Serves 1**

Mushrooms Provençal

Put the oil in a glass bowl with the onion, garlic, herbs and seasoning. Cover with a glass plate and cook on High for 2 minutes. Stir in the tomatoes and mushrooms. Cover and cook on High for 4 minutes, stirring halfway through the cooking. Serve with the tagliatelle. **Serves 4-6**

Right: Mushrooms Provençal.

INGREDIENTS

4 medium-sized baking potatoes
1 tablespoon oil
1 clove garlic, crushed
½ pound brown mushrooms, sliced
2 slices bacon, chopped
1 tablespoon dried chives

✤

2 large white mushrooms
2 small eggs
2 tablespoons milk
1 tablespoon butter, cut into four pieces
1 slice toast

✤

1 tablespoon oil
1 large onion, finely chopped
1 clove garlic, crushed
½ teaspoon mixed fresh thyme and sage, chopped
4 large ripe tomatoes, peeled, halved, seeded and finely chopped
1 pound small button mushrooms, halved
½ pound tagliatelle, cooked and drained

Savory mushrooms

Put the butter in a small glass dish, and cook on Medium for 45 seconds. Remove the tips of the mushroom stalks, and chop them finely. Put the mushroom caps in a large glass dish. Make the bread into crumbs, and put into a bowl with the mushroom stalks, herbs, half the garlic, ham, cheese and seasoning. Bind with the egg and about a third of the melted butter.

Divide the stuffing among the mushroom caps. Add the remaining garlic to the remaining butter, and pour over the mushrooms. Cook on High for 5-6 minutes depending on the size of mushrooms. Serve on toast, garnished with tomatoes. **Serves 4**

Creamed mushrooms

Melt the butter on High for ½ minute. Add the mushrooms, and cook on High for 2 minutes, stirring after 1 minute. Blend together the sour cream, mustard, Worcestershire sauce, and tomato paste. Stir the mixture into the mushrooms. Cook on Low for 3 minutes until thoroughly heated, but do not allow to boil. Season to taste, garnish with oregano, and serve with wholewheat toast as a snack. **Serves 4**

Light mushroom soup

Cook the butter in a 1½-quart glass bowl on High for 1 minute. Add the onion and mushrooms, and stir well to coat with the butter. Cover, and cook on High for 5 minutes. Stir in the milk, stock, potato, nutmeg and seasoning. Cover, and cook on High for 10 minutes. Purée in a blender, and stir in the cream. Cook on Medium for 1 minute. Serve hot or chilled. **Serves 6**

Top left: Light mushroom soup; Savory mushrooms (top right);
Creamed mushrooms (bottom).

INGREDIENTS

½ cup butter
8 large white mushrooms
3-4 slices brown or white bread
2 tablespoons chopped parsley
½ teaspoon fresh rosemary
2 cloves garlic, crushed
¾ cup finely chopped ham
⅓ cup grated Cheddar cheese
1 medium egg
8 rounds of toast

1 tablespoon butter
¾ pound medium button mushrooms,
thickly sliced
⅔ cup sour cream
1½ teaspoons whole-grain mustard
1 tablespoon Worcestershire sauce
1 tablespoon tomato paste
toast

2 tablespoons butter
1 onion, chopped
1 pound medium button mushrooms,
chopped
2 cups skimmed milk
1¼ cups chicken stock
⅔ cup chopped potato
½ teaspoon ground nutmeg
⅔ cup light cream

Trout in creamy mushroom and celery sauce

Put the oil and celery into a glass mixing bowl. Cover with a glass plate. Cook on High for 2 minutes. Stir in the mushrooms, cover, and cook on High for a further 3 minutes. Stir in the chopped tarragon and grated lemon peel. Stir in the sour cream and seasoning gradually.

Arrange the trout in a shallow dish, put a sprig of tarragon and slice of lemon inside each trout, then cover with the mushroom mixture. Cover, and cook on Medium for 20 minutes, turning after 10 minutes. Stand for 3 minutes before serving with new potatoes and green beans. **Serves 4**

Salmon steaks in mushroom sauce

Put the flour in a glass bowl, and mix in the milk gradually, first making a smooth paste, then adding it more quickly, and whisking all the time. Add the bay leaf, mace, seasoning and butter. Cook on High for 7-10 minutes until the sauce has boiled and thickened, whisking once halfway through the cooking time. Add the mushrooms, and cook on High for a further minute. Cover, and keep warm.

Cook the salmon steaks, covered, on High for 8 minutes. Stand for 5 minutes. Reheat the sauce for 1-2 minutes, and pour around the fish. Garnish with lemon and parsley. **Serves 4**

Right: Salmon steaks in mushroom sauce.

INGREDIENTS

1 tablespoon oil
3 stalks celery, finely chopped
½ pound medium button mushrooms, sliced
2 tablespoons chopped fresh tarragon
grated peel of 1 large lemon
⅔ cup sour cream
4 (¾-pound) trout, cleaned
4 sprigs fresh tarragon
4 slices lemon

❦

4 tablespoons all-purpose flour
2½ cups milk
1 bay leaf
blade of mace
2 tablespoons butter
½ pound small button mushrooms
4 salmon steaks
GARNISH
lemon
parsley

❦

Coq au vin

Put the oil, garlic and shallots into a large glass bowl. Cover, and cook on High for 1 minute. Add the bacon, and cook on High for a further minute. Add the mushrooms, stir well, and cook on High for 2 minutes. Pour over the wine and chicken stock, and add the bouquet garni. Coat the chicken drumsticks in the flour, and arrange in a separate glass dish. Cook the chicken, uncovered, on High for 8 minutes. Pour over the wine and mushroom mixture. Cover and cook on High for 6 minutes, then on Low for 30 minutes, stirring once halfway through the cooking time. If the chicken is not tender, cook, covered, on Low for a further 10 minutes. Stand for 5 minutes before serving garnished with chopped parsley. **Serves 4**

Mushroom and cauliflower au gratin

Put the cauliflower florets into a large glass bowl. Add 3 tablespoons hot water. Cover, and cook on High for 12 minutes. Set aside. Meanwhile, put the mushrooms and butter into a glass cup, and cook on High for 3 minutes. Strain the water from the cauliflower. Add the mushrooms to the cauliflower, reserving the butter and juices in the cup. Add the flour and mustard to the cup, and whisk in the milk. Cook on High for 3 minutes, stirring once during the cooking time. Add the cheese, stir well, then pour over the cauliflower and mushrooms. Cook, uncovered, on High for 5 minutes. **Serves 4**

Left: Mushroom and cauliflower au gratin; Coq au vin (right).

INGREDIENTS

1 tablespoon oil
1 clove garlic, finely chopped
8 shallots
4 slices bacon, chopped
¾ pound small button mushrooms
2 cups red wine
⅔ cup hot chicken stock
bouquet garni
8 chicken drumsticks
2 tablespoons all-purpose flour
GARNISH
chopped parsley

~

1 medium cauliflower, broken into florets
¾ pound brown mushrooms, sliced
¼ cup butter
3 tablespoons all-purpose flour
1 teaspoon mustard powder
1 cup milk
⅓ cup grated Cheddar cheese

~

Index

Acknowledgments

The author and publishers would like to thank the following chefs for supplying recipes for inclusion in the book: Richard Williamson, of the Portman Hotel, London, England (Sauté of specialty mushrooms); André Wintergill, of the Royal Bath Hotel, Bournemouth, England (Mushroom and salmon molds with lentils); Tina Walsh, of the Lacken House Restaurant, Kilkenny, Eire (Mille feuille of mushrooms).